Litany
for Wound and Bloom

Litany
for Wound and Bloom

Poems

Judith H. Montgomery

First U.S. edition 2018

Editor and Publisher   Laura LeHew

Proofreaders: Quinton Hallett
Nancy Carol Moody

Cover Art: "Abstract relief texture in red and blue"
© Matahiasek | Dreamstime.com

Copyright © 2018 Judith H. Montgomery

All Rights Reserved. Except for brief passages quoted in a newspaper, magazine, radio or television review, no portion of this book may be reproduced in any form or by any means, electronic or mechanical, including photocopying and recording, or by any information storage and retrieval system, without written permission from the Publisher. All rights to the works printed herein remain with the author.

ISBN: 978-0-9998334-1-4

Uttered Chaos
PO Box 50638
Eugene, OR 97405
www.utteredchaos.org

For

>My dear sons
>Alexander and Andrew

And for

>Inspiring poet, mentor, and friend
>Maxine Scates

Table of Contents

I (Womb)

What Were You, Before 1

Apoptosis 2

Expectant: I 3

Fields, Burning 4

D & C 5

Cicatricula 6

Echo Baby Blue 9

Yet Praise the Scar 12

Expectant: II 13

Ultra/Sounding 14

Night Terrors 15

Waiting Room 16

B-Word 17

II (Word)

Having Vanished 23

Resistance 25

Her Silence Is 27

Listen 28

Black Seed 30

Inflorescence 33

Advice: to Demeter 35

Sometimes 36

Kneeling 38

Tomoko Uemura and Her Mother in the Bath 40

Breast: Still 43

Another Kind of Prayer 45

III (Witness)

- Bearing/Bearing Down 51
- Follow-through 53
- Proper 55
- A Blessing, ... 57
- *Gassed* 59
- Yellow Jacket 61
- Simmer 62
- Hostage Clock 64
- The Coat 65
- Five Ways to Wear the Balaclava 66
- But You My Son 68
- *Send* 70

ACKNOWLEDGMENTS 75
NOTES 78
BIO 80

I
(Womb)

What Were You, Before

you slipped into your flesh suit,
its rosy padding, and zipped it up,

little latch throbbing in your throat?
Slide of light, sip of mother blood-

breath? Until you loosed the pulsing
cord to swim into this next world—

passage to desire. Incarnate, yield
to succulence and savor—crush

of almond marzipan upon the tongue,
ooze of cool mud between toes

in August's sweat-dogged days,
even blood's salt sting licked from

the paper cut—all addictive. Once
elected, there's no turning back from

the body's habit, which is to say,
habitation, package wrapping that

first sip or slide, earth-lured and fiercely
clinging to vessel, to bone and flesh—

bloomed, wounded—harried, healed—
willing neither to perish, nor to pine

for the bland and dimming memory of Paradise.

Apoptosis

Every month her body prepares the scarlet garden,
leaf on leaf of nesting cells to plump the shelter,

rich red bed stitched with spiral-arteries ready
to bear gifts to feed the visitor. And every

month one packed golden drop releases, lit seed
slipping down the sleek chute until that fortunate

fall into the womb's open heart, its come-hither
welcome to the brave egg yearning for anchor.

But this time or that the pursed lip of ovary locks
the egg in place, or this time or that the sperm loll

and perish, drugged away from match. A chilled
breath begins to frost the unsettled center. The nest

blebs, falters, looses its hold. Leaf-fall begins. Wind
sweeps the garden bare. There is no baby in this poem.

Expectant: I

They drape the splendid
    hood down my honored spine:

it drags my bent neck
    back. High-degree'd at last, I

am delivered of a paper-
    white palimpsest of words.

Bless these letters—
    appendage to identity—

they re-christen me in fine-
    point pen. But this black

sack edged in peacock
    velvet, lined in flame:

an empty shimmer,
    a placental mockery—

counter to the bone
    desert of my pelvis, its

alkaline flats, its cradle
    of refusal—banked ashes

in the mouth of Judith:
    which means *praised. Praised.*

And *barren.*

Fields, Burning

       I envy these fields, consuming
down to carbon: burnt back to start
    fresh at dirt and root . . .
                 half-masked
in smoke, three men dip drip-torches
    low to flame the mowed acres close,
close, beside my car as I drive home
    to bitter blue.
            Aftermath: there's
the word: green shoots that break
    through char, rise after swath and match
have finished off this year's chaff.

Rough August wind roils the fields,
    blooms smoke across my line of sight.
I pump the brakes, not wanting to crash.
    Or to return too fast . . .
                 what if I pulled
over, stopped, hidden inside
    this veil? Listened. Would every
thing burn clear?
            I kill the engine, float.
    If I swing the door wide, step out
into this field of refining fire . . . no
    path forward, back:
             what if the way
      is *through*?

D & C

Duck and cover, she thinks when the doctor
speaks—and she flickers to first-grade,

girls and boys wild as squirrels, diving
under shelter of the child-sized desks,

bloodhearts whumping, while high in the hot
dry sky above their school invisible planes

begin to buzz, ready to loose the terrible
swift bombs from which the scarred desks

are to save them—but she's avoiding
her sentence, she hauls her mind to bear

(what her body will not do) on his words,
on his manicured hands that wave above

the desk he keeps between them, far from
the growths that salt her womb. *Standard*

procedure, he repeats, impatient with her
weeping. Dismissed to search out the nurse,

she sets a date for this invasion. *Dilation*
and curettage, a cutting meant to cure her

barrenness. To bloom, she understands,
first she must be wounded.

Cicatricula

Whetted instruments
slung at my hip,

hands ungloved
to best tend

to spent stalk and blossom,
I am caught

between *bloom* and *prune*,
my will imposed on the wild.

...

Even before
the scarlet snips

approach a drooping stem,
the blood-red

geranium
has sealed the sap

from this leaf
or that. Falling

away, it marks
the mother.

...

Cicatricula:
little scars nicked

as each egg departs
the round dock of ovary

to undertake the great
dazed journey

to the womb.
To fusion, bloom.

      ...

Behind, a mending—
a century of welts

hatching and cross-
hatching, a thicket

of lost launchings.

      ...

Behind, apparently
nothing. No

raw wound
a skilled surgeon

might repair—
merely an historical

record of embrace
and rupture, of

turning away.

      ...

Not one scarlet drop
seeps from these

seams. As no drop
will seep

seen by any eye
when each sweet

one releases,
engraving scars

of which no one
but the woman

will speak.

ECHO BABY BLUE
— for C.

Blue's how baby eyes begin.
Even yours set to blue because you're
    two four six eight   multiplying cells
but bent and busted, baby-buggy
    stopped too quick off centerline.
Sweet kiddo, who would not hum
    straight into my waiting womb.
Caught, stuck in the Fallopian chute.
    Ectopic. So they tell me while we
watch you on the ultrasound, docked
    and riding out ripples busy busy getting
ready to be

    . . .

    my baby   you, a shimmy in
the spotlight. I play brave as any good
    girl staring down the needle stuck into
my skin   letting mr. methotrexate in—
    your name, *Kate*, on his calling card.
To get you   before you get me. Me
    a little bit pregnant   one more night.
Go home they say, *call us when,*
    press cotton tight to the needle-hole
so mr. methotrex   AKA death   can't
    slide back

    . . .

    out   *Do you have some body?*
they ask me. I say *sure*   not telling
    he said *bye, baby*. . . . Now, home,
pet rabbit nibbles by my shoes.
    I can cradle her—she's not the one
who's dead   but doesn't know it . . .
    now mr. death slipslides, top hat
and tails—your Fred Astaire tap
    tapping past each rib, dance
card in his hand . . . says

. . .

    may I have this . . . they made me
hold out my ice arm where he
  could begin his tango to the tube.
Check for blood they said. *Call
  us if. Call us when.* But no spotted
cotton. O sweetrunt *Katy Kate*
  don't make me   choose—
I have to lose you, loose
  you have to

. . .

   come back in. They measure
out my blood. *Not yet.* Insist
  admission. I admit nothing
but mr. death. Every girlname tastes
  of ash and cigarette. The nurse not
looking at the white line that's
  my mouth *not trembling* . . . holds
out the slitted gown. They lie me
  lie us

. . .

   down to snake plastic tubes
in for lull-a-bye sleep-eggs
  sliding down the bottle vein
suckblip *blip* here we go
  'round the mulberry *ashes ashes
all fall down ring-around-the
   rosy* where my mama untied
me   cut/uncut too-

. . .

   soon baby gloved and white-tie'd
doctors two-step tip-tap echo
  ice-light *mothermayI have this*

lullaby   *baby* only   one of us
        can curtsey   off   this dancefloor
count down
       they tell me

                . . .

      and I
   one   *hundred*   oh   *ninety-*
        nine   oh   soon   we'll not
be pregnant any   not

       even   a little   *ninety-*
          ninety-
oh blue-baby
            you can't count
   on me
       no more

YET PRAISE THE SCAR

    Consider how, breached by blade
or flame, the body rushes to repair,
        quick-clot the hurt. Fibers stitch

    swift to shut inviolate the gape
of flesh. Such fierce haste to mend,
        but not what we'd call *grace*—

    the awkward seam puckers up, cross-
linked ridge of collagen contracting
        stung flesh. Each scar an X'd fence

    of barbs that interrupts the seamless
landscape of saved skin. Yet even
        itching, aching—tender to the thumb—

    each scar's a scarlet witness on or
in the body, inscribing its stubborn
        devotion: *Hurt. Hurry. Heal.*

EXPECTANT: II

Quickening at last, I lay
    the heavy hood away—
        break out, white sail

wind-hovering. This
    swollen belly prowing
        passage: at last fruitful.

Now my body speaks,
    my bloom proclaims
        before me: who

and why I am—re-baptized
    in the name of this father,
        this son and the holy . . .

anointed, myrrh'd and
    honey'd, in silence I scribe
        hypnotic reams of names—

Alexander, Nicholas—
    James, William, Andrew—
        I am what I am   become—

the word made flesh,
    preparing to spill forth.
        Unfurling each rib, I enter

hallow, from *hollow*,
    not *scholar*, but *mother*—
        Judith, body-blessed.

Ultra/Sounding

Dear Not-Daughter: How could you spurn me—
whip your tail less frantic than your brother
jousting boisterous up the corridor
to pitch woo in the diamond of my womb?

For you, I would have gemmed my egg
in Fabergé, released the corsets
of the cervix, and wrapped you in a fond
Fallopian embrace, cradled in pink dark.

I knit caps of down to shield your fontanelle—
you cast off in a spray of osprey feathers.
Daughter, do you wander me, aswim in vein
or artery? In possibility. Do you ripple

at my rib or wing my breath?—my Icara
off-course and falling, almost fertile, in me.

...

But—*Mother-Waiting*—You sigh: I'm blown
rib to rib—answer, hummingbird to heel,
leaf to breath. Your longing melts the wax
that wings me. Jams my radar blind. I'm

not daughter. Not dawdler. But called to read
your body's book: to set plumbline to spine,
to round the syllables of ball-and-socket.
You my home-school, I your pupil-star.

Curie. Curator. And ready medic, mother:
Nightingale with bandage to your bone.
You'd call me to release my rounds,
bend to birth—would you relinquish flight

for flesh? for me? Here find no *Never-Girl*,
but Icara—glider, keeper. Let me be.

Night Terrors

He is standing, screaming. Shaking
the rail of the blue-shadowed crib

again. Eyes, glazed. Opaque.
Open, but not to you or the lop-

eared rabbit or the paper-folded bird
gliding white above the nursery lamp.

His body is hostage to a phantom
horse that tangles his wrists in reins,

and drags him deep into alien terrain.
You cannot wake him to your breast.

Rush him wailing from the house,
plunge into the moon-sharp street

where elms splay black in March
and bare feet burn on frost. Talk

him back from the terror—not
knowing what he's seen. Your night-

gown whips your knees. Words
clack and shatter on the ice-slick walk.

You would do *anything*—
gas and flame your library of books,

renounce the earth and its green rustle
of bright sun—whatever

it takes to fetch him home.

Waiting Room

> *To write, one needs only a pen. Of course,
> by pen I mean enclosure.*
> —Heather McGowan, *Schooling*

The young woman in the peach tunic—
its pebbled weave soft as baby yarn,

pearl buttons perfect as a line of moons—
rests her tablet of words on the enormous

world that plumps beneath her breasts,
that rises like a Rosa peach before her.

I've been in the body of this body. Know
how it listens to itself, rapt on ripening.

Wholly tuned to the hungry fruit that
presses a tunic open at the hem, not

knowing how an unexpected fissure
might wait ahead, how the body will fall—

as mine did—in love with the rosy body
of her child.   And release the pen.

Pages I had written, pages I'd expected
to write—washed in milk and blood,

swept up post-delivery. I tuned my ear
to whimper, called away from word.

Will she also shift from pen to play-
pen—overwhelmed by the demanding

grammar of her child's cries? I could
be wrong. Perhaps she writes a letter

to her lover. Perhaps she will not miss
the pen, swapping lines for lullaby. For

her, the other pen might be enough.

B-Word

—after the Brussels bombings, March 22, 2016
—after a line by Joy Katz

1

Some words cannot breach the box of the poem.

2

Box may be admitted, as in boxing match.
Or box of matches. Bomb, as in Brussels.
Put a b___ in a poem, and watch it . . .

blast. Bodies littering a shattered airport
(apartment, corner deli . . .) floor. Breached
security, then bleed-out. Bandage: blanket

grabbed to wrap a burned body. Because
break. Blow. Boast. Border. Brothers.
Brandish. Bang. And body count.

The territory of the poem confiscated by
genes that read XY XY XY: Boy. Who
clutches the ball—or was it bomb?—beneath

one arm, as he batters shouting to the goal.

3

Some words bawl into the basket of the poem.

4

Birth. Breech. Breast. Belly, blooming.
    Put a b___ in a poem, watch
it fall. . . .Bubble. Bib. Bawl. Balm.
    Stoppage of monthly blood,
that impure evidence. Not
        Mary *immaculata.*

Proscription: no kid, no pup, no apple
    of the eye. *Put a b___ in the poem, and watch*

it fall like a stone . . .
                No diaper. No shit. No fond toddle—
no bless, no bliss. No public cradling
        of the lively arrival.

No X and O, kiss and cuddle, no
        voicing by the body bearing two Xs
wound in the promise of the double spiral.
        No as though to blot out

the body of the *baby. Put a baby in a poem*
        and watch it fall, like a stone
through wet tissue.
                We body forth no stones,
        but manuscripts of genes,
scrolls intricately sheltered in the blanket
        of blood and balm.

        Birth: origin of every one of us, XX,
XY. Bidden, not forbidden, words
        called to celebrate every messy
entrance. Embodiment. I *will*
        bring a baby into this world
of (war) (wrath) words.

        5

All words uncoil to bloom in the womb of the poem.

II

(Word)

Having Vanished

In the beginning was the Word...

Each molecule of air shines—
        the angel having vanished—

and a skirt of shimmer
        flicks off dust-dried walls,

scuffed floor. Each shadow
        lies: angled, obedient. This

room, apparently empty. Yet
        no room is wholly bare, where

messengers appear. Who
        flame the air with feathers

to deliver holy words in ears.
        Bright-blinded, the woman

has felt her way along the wall,
        not yet grasping that *Exit* is

out of any question. Her plain
        cloak hazes toward cerulean.

Slow motes glitter in a slide
        of light, restless behind her

fleeing feet. Yet she pauses, turns
        back to look. Half-in, half-out

the salt threshold. Her womb,
        no longer hers, filling. Filled.

This ambiguous gift: crossed
        in cords of thorn. Delivered.

Yet to be delivered. Suspended
        at the sill, she strokes a brush-

burn—one departing wing's
        careless lash on her bare wrist—

as though she'd been branded.
        Claimed. Nothing lies empty

here: not the numinous chamber,
        not the redbudburst of her womb,

nor the seared box of her heart,
        which flutters its singed petals

like sparrow wings—frantic,
        netted. Only the angel escapes.

Resistance

after "Arab Woman" (1905-06)
—John Singer Sargent

Mark how he's blurred her face—
    smudged blue, mute, as he paints

her   still   into our dazzled
    gaze— she apparently gazeless,

anonymous— face erased above
    a body veiled head to ankle,

arch aswirl in cream and blue-
    shadowed cloth— such delectable

drape— his paint containing what
    what   as he takes her measure—

as she braces against stroke
    and sanding sirocco— resists

the touch of his sable brush   laying
    caress   of shadow, flare   of sun—

and despite   the dry gusts
    that against her limbs press

this lush swath   which hides
    but does not hide   her shape—

which threatens to whip away,
    revealing what   *what*   as she

faces— faces down any eye—
    mark how she anchors against

knowing, counters embrace—
    cloth knotted tight in a hidden

fist, she asks for nothing,
    gives away nothing— speaks

and withstands
    by the firm holdfast of her hand.

Her Silence Is

endless linen wound to cripple
        her toes, binding ever closer

the voices of her feet. Her hair
        bound in a snood of woven gold.

    Is statement. Custom. Consequence.

Her hips' swash constricted
        by panniers' brocade. Floating

rib removed, the more closely
        to corset her waist. Breath.

    Is handcuff. Straitjacket. Gag.

Her stiletto heel. Hobble-skirt. Chador
        muting verb and adverb of her stride.

Both bandage and wound. Glitter
        and mesh that nets her tongue.

    Is calling. Witness. Refusal.

Is shame. Cinch: apron string, crib.
        Is fear: of what she might say,

were she free to speak: breaking
        forth from ankle, ear, hair, cheek,

rib   hand   hip   lip   lips—
        breaking forth from tongue

        tongue   unbridled tongue

Listen

If the moon had been tatter and fog
    (but the night air was sharp and clear)—

if I lived in green valleys of wheat
    (but I live on this cratered square)—

    . . .

I'd have unlocked the courtyard door
    to my son's sweet, impatient face,

his white sleeves rolled to the elbow,
    hands bearing the evening bread, the wine—

    . . .

If the moon had been tatter and fog
    if we lived in green valleys of wheat—

the crowd might have missed the cap,
    the accent, the mark that betrayed him,

might have followed their guttering torches
    to crush another's ripe seed—

    . . .

(*Listen*: I thought that my son, like others',
    was destined to see me to sleep,

to light the memorial candle,
    to lift his voice to honor my name—)

    . . .

(but the night air was sharp and clear)—
    (but we live on this cratered square)—

What I heard . . . a brute noise,
    a breaking. I snatched at the door—so—

and saw, not my child bearing blessing,
    but the mob, like teeth as they took him,

in this square, on this stone-littered street,
    with no alley, no route for escape—

       ...

If the moon had been tatter and fog
    (but the night air was sharp and clear)—

they broke him with cobble and board,
    shattered his bones with a plank,

pinned me fast to the courtyard gate . . .

       ...

If we'd lived in green valleys of wheat
    (but I live, if it's live, on this square)—

they turned me to watch. (The bread
    stained red. The wine spilled,

bile on shale.) Forced me to watch
    as he drowned

in the bitter lake of bad blood.

       ...

If the moon had been . . .

Black Seed

Poppies brought him—scarlet caught up
        in the basket of my apron—more
                delicious than narcissus' waxy flutes.

My right hand, reckless, sought a second
        flamed bloom, its dab of deckled gold, its
                bottomless black velvet cup. Dragon-

flies were gilding river air when Mother
        turned aside to stroke the cornsilk rippling
                beneath her smile. When I licked pollen

    from my thumb, the breeze rang with hooves.

        . . .

I cried out,
        poppies spilling from my lap.
                They could not say I went willing—

the sinew hoop of his arm ringed
        my ribs, corralled a heart that leapt
                and leapt, but could not lift my body back

to sky. Parting cornstalks rolled above
        my brow—Mother's hand, bloody with burst
                petals, slipped from my unwinding hair.

        . . .

Silver filter. Echo. Moon sliced by
        stalactite. In the flicker of the torch
                propped in Charon's prow, I untie

my white apron, let it fall away. Drink
        the river-whisper scuffing earth voices
                under shade. Caught in my shift, a birch

twig rimes. My spine—stiffening with ice.
        Not yet do I look on Hades' face.

                . . .

And yet. This spill of ruby blooming
        at my step. Oil of almond that anoints
                lobe and lip. A ravishing that strikes

my body's net of lightning—as pale
        wraiths stream, murmuring through gates
                of smoke. I plait a crown of asphodel,

bracelet of black tulip. Bathe wrist
        and thigh in attar of rose. I am Queen
                of Night, voice of nightshade dreaming,

who seals her ear against reprieve. Blood-
        songs well from palm and throat . . .
                this liquor that burns and wounds:

        I crave the only cup.

                . . .

But burning's not enough to drown
        the other world—Mother pleads before
                the gods' thrones, how I am stolen,

how thistles stalk her drooping fields.
        My Lord pulls from his side a gleaming
                mirror, spins it into *skiff, stallion, ladder*.

Groaning for his gaze, I will take
        no escape. From my breast, a crimson scarf
                he knots into a glowing fruit. Its skin

licks mine: at its heart, scarlet seeds singed
        black. Black. But seeds.

...

I *will* eat. Swallow: and Mother's cries
        split flame-wavering walls. My wrists
                shed onyx petals, my wreath ashes over.

I must re-cover my self: bind in snood
        and apron to be suitable for sun. I fight
                the rise: they could not say I went, willing.

Snatched to earth where mere robins
        stitch leaves tight to docile trees. Again:
                daughter who kneels weeping at her

joyful mother's feet. Obediently seeded
        back into her heart. Whose hoe awaits
                this daughter's hand, tender of sun-

        sweetened rows of corn. Corn. But rows.

...

Rocked, ripe. Lap full of late pods
        to snap, almost content, I loose the green
                shower of peas into the wooden bowl—

but one, seared black, lingers in my palm.
        Tempting as the pomegranate's
                shining fist of seeds. How bones ache

for that lost place. How this body longs
        to shed the sun's white sack. Tomorrow,
                by the poppy drift, I'll pick the pollen-

        loaded blooms. Tune my woman's ear to hooves.

INFLORESCENCE

Lost Aunt Lucille, whose name never licked
across my mother's lips for forty of my years—

only now I hear you were erased in a scarlet blaze
of fever, four-year-old singed by interloping fire.

Scarlatina—inflorescing flame that lit your flesh
until you gleamed against the sweat-sheeted

toddler's bed. Coals glowed in your body's tinder
box. Your parched throat fluttered in smoke.

Your flexible bones that served as heart's shield
and ladder, blistered in a last configuration. . . .

Shadow-aunt, who might have softened my grand-
father's heart that beat only for a boy—girl who

might have huddled with her older sister, starved
together for that word of love reserved for the later-

born heir—at last your name rising from my
mother's paling memory, as we pause in the deserted

nursery to choose among tissue-paper bulbs to plant
for spring. My mother gathers fists of daffodils

succulently stored, but resists the heaped hyacinths
that I adore—intoxicating fragrance, petal-cluster,

velvet perfume rush. . . . You would this day have
been eighty-two and fraying, perhaps limping down

a garden path of violet hyacinths as they turn perfect
petals to drink in the blazing and distant sun. . . .

Lucille, twice lost—once to scorching fever, once
to love and history—at last I can imagine you,

tucked in a Sunday-white lace-budded dress in your
white tiny coffin, the heavy-headed hyacinths nodding

in stained light that streams through the Glenburn
parish church. And my mother—sniffling in her

child's hanky—choked on drafts of cloying scent
that might have covered the bitter odor of fire,

which ravishes, like love, only where it glances.

ADVICE: TO DEMETER

Open the envelope of dream.

Do not turn back:
fog curtains the bed,

and moon glances off
the sleep-shuttered house.

Enter the acres of blaze.

As before, crownfire
leaps from the needles,

ravages your throat.
Beargrass flares underfoot.

Your seared soles—
unbearable. The thought

of your daughter
corralled in flame—not bearable.

Do not struggle against smoke—

breathe it in, make it yours,
make it bearable.

If again you put on
the spiked crown of fire—

if, barefooted, you descend
the burning ridge—

you may open for your daughter
a shelter on damp moss,

a path of green breath
she will take to escape

the blue flame you've become.

Sometimes

An indigo cloak clasped at her paper throat,
my mother is stepping

deep and deeper into a mute forest wing-lit with
birds, a basket of seeds

clutched in her hand. Once in a while, she
remembers

and scoops deep into the swirl—and gathers
a handful to sow

all about her, strewing the path with her time-
tested mix of dun

pearls of millet, of Ethiopian nyjer tiny as
rice, the richest black-

oil sunflower seeds—and so making a feast
under her feet, to delight

the rose-breasted house finches, arrow-tailed
swifts, her juncos,

her mourning doves calling *where are you
where are you* as they

alight, as they light her path into thickening
woods. Sometimes,

she stops, to consider the narrowing way—
to right and left,

storm-felled trunks stitched with swordfern
and moss, straddled

by opportune alder. Ahead, a dim bramble
of brush. Sometimes,

my mother looks back, turns around, around,
slippered feet tentative

over awkward ground laced with uneven
root-wad and rock

under drifts of soft duff. A vine maple's
reddened and

tumbling leaves brush her wrist, and she stops
to point out the flutter,

color and call of so many birds to my father,
although he is not

on the path she follows into the tangled
heart of the forest,

close and damp after rain. These woods—
vines and branches, holes

and encroaching thickets—hers alone, where he
cannot follow. . . . Now streaking

the dusk, one cardinal flares, far from their
New England home—

scarlet-headed and cloaked, plump ensign
who darts in and out

of the cumulate dark, to light on her shoulder—
and she feels how she flies

wordless under his heart, how she enters his heart,
and he hers.

She picks up the basket, steps on into twilight—
the cardinal weeping,

his red breast sweeping and lighting the one-
way one way.

Kneeling

Her ankles. Toes. Her yellowing nails:
       groove lunula hallux. I bend
to my basin, its warming pour, its
       attar of lavender . . .

Kneel: to unlace the stiff shoes   to slip
       cuffed socks   roll up the slacks   her
flesh: calves indented. Cinctured. Rough-
       reddened joints . . .

       . . .

Her vessel   of days: its thirty-one thousand
       drops.   *Mother. Daughter* . . . the swelling
nights: who cradled my crown
       under her ribs . . .

Who   in the darkened cinema   shed
       her shoes   *Shall We Dance?*   barefooted
not counting edema: gather of waters.
       Her weeping . . .

       . . .

I gather her arch   her heel   her proud ankle
       once slim as a wrist. The twenty-six thin-
worn bones of the foot. Their intricate
       joinery. Journey . . .

You are—   *my daughter?* Salt scrub.
       Infusion of bergamot. Not yet translucent:
her thinning skin. Urge the trapped fluid
       back   to the heart . . .

       . . .

In the yielding towel   cradle each instep . . .
       Ginger and Fred. We showed off our steps
at the dance . . . where is   *your father?*
       This synapse   also

unmooring . . . tranced   she closes
       her eyes   dreams under skin steeped
in sunned aloe lotion   who could not honor
      such rapture. . . ?

             . . .

Seized up in delight   she opens, strokes—
      her hand   my cheek. *You: my
daughter. Such*
        a good daughter.

Tomoko Uemura and Her Mother in the Bath

after a photograph (December 1971)
—W. Eugene Smith

1 Ofuro: The Soaking Tub

      The *ofuro* has been filled.
Its wooden walls and gathered water
         appear dark as spilled oil. What
we can see is permitted only by light
         that lights on flesh, a white-wrapped
head, a rise of bones exposed. Axis
         of shock and beauty, stamped
in black and white.

2 Tomoko Uemura: Daughter

Floating, supported in her mother's
    arms, the two
        bodies crossed in eloquent
echo. Look and look
        away from this Pietà—
   from contorted form—
            the naked and damaged
daughter—at 15, ever breastless.
    Whose ribs plainly strain
            beneath her taut
skin. Whose hands
    warp at fingers, wrist.
   Tomoko peers back, as
though to counter, or
      encounter
           the photographer,
her image floating
    in the glass
        of his lens.

3 Chisso-Minamata byō: Chisso-Minamata Disease

1956: her birth.   1977: her death.

    . . . the placenta removes [methyl-mercury]
    from the mother's bloodstream. . . concentrates

the chemical in the fetus. . . . [Chisso Company's]
own tests revealed that its wastewater contained
many heavy metals . . . discharged directly
into Minamata River. . . .

Water she absorbed
    in the womb. Water in which she bathes—
no, *is* bathed—
        before us.

When the mothers protested, the fathers—
    those who could still
        speak. To those who knew.
The O,O of their cries—
            denied.

4 *Ryoko Uemura: Mother*

. . . who chose place and pose, a deliberate
    testament to doubled suffering. Who exposes
and enfolds her child in witness
    that cannot be distinguished
        from love.
            She bares and bears
again Tomoko's weight, light catching
    the swell of her own
            flawless flesh—
smoothed shoulder, hint of breast—
    and the crisp scarf wrapped
about her head.
        Lit, the arc of her wrist as she lifts
    her daughter's legs into lens-
range, so that injury
        may be made   plain
            to those with eyes to see. . . .

And yet, beyond what shock
        the flash discloses,
    its light falls almost softly   on this mother's
face   as she bends her gaze to her child,

                    not afraid to look
            on what's gone wrong.
                        She holds her daughter's body
afloat in black waters,   so that we may see
                how beauty and despair are leavened by
            the fiercest love
                            that dares exposure.
                                    See, she says, without
looking our way. *What has
            been done.   What we endure.*

Breast: Still

after a photograph, "Beauty out of Damage"
—self-portrait by Matuschka (1993)

Her breasts sloped
under silk,

ripened as nectarines
ripen to brandy.

Now a ladder of sutures
brands the chest

she bares for the cool
eye of her lens.

We are invited to look
at the dark

spring of curl at her nape.
Rose arc of cheek.

Delicate
embroidery of bones.

She turns her gaze
out of the frame

that we may hold her
in our hands

and trace, unnoticed,
the new welt of seam.

Still, the deliberate
line of her jaw lifts

out of shadow. Still,
falling through the picture,

the ivory gown
chooses its curve—

framing the not-breast
so we may see it

for what it is: more
than the nebula

burst in the mammogram—
more than a gene's crooked stitch.

See, the artist says,
it's gone.

A sharp needle's mended loss
across her rib—still

she summons us to see
beyond absent beauty

to bloom of lip,
to pulse of nectar at her throat—

to all that speaks, and lives.

ANOTHER KIND OF PRAYER

Naked before   a mirror bright as winter water
      I assess the swell   breast, breast, hip and hip—
then stroke   across my ribs   flesh peppered
      in rough   impurities   not tumors   just
excrescences of skin   so like those freckling
      my father's abdomen   as he let his body slip
inside the hot tub's healing waters—   so that for a short
      space of time   he could ease away   the burden
of mothering my mother—
              who is it I am
becoming?   and shamed by my desire to be
my father   and not to be my mother—whose
      words have fled   whose sapped flesh is all
that remains   who is   dewording   as a pond
      may be dewatered—   exposing drowned debris
pondweed   white-bellied bass   one rusted
      shopping cart   mute   histories of what was
once   but is no longer   attached to any story.

      If   *in the beginning was the Word*   then what
of ending—   *stutter?* then   *silence?*   even
      now   or tomorrow   while I bend to kiss her
cheek   rub her cracked heels   with oil of almond
      my mind flails against   what fated inheritance—
I rewrite   my unfolding story
              to read how I
am all father   I embrace his intermittent

heart— it is my heart   his warped iris is
      the glass that swerves my sight—   his heritable blood
beats inside my veins—   but do not admit
      my mother's heavy breasts   her wiped beauty   her
failing tongue   she who floated me   inside
      the bowl of her body   borne through winter ice

how could I wish   now to wince away   her
      genes?—   fearing her story mine and staring into
mirrors   knowing   as she has a knowing
      of what vanishes   water leaking   out of its basin
and weeping—
          how to live inside such terrible. . . .
     I bend to bathe her feet   as though to bandage
an unacknowledged wound   with my hair I would
      wipe each arch   lavish there the balm of costly
oils—   penitence
          penance   for such dark
     and naked   such terrible   wishing.

III

(Witness)

BEARING/BEARING DOWN

They measure the center
for *centimeter* and *effacement*—then say *push*,

Anglo-Saxon, firm, *do
this*—even while the body's hard at work,

panting—its nerved-up
muscles squeeze to speed the quickened burden

down the birth canal.
Then: lifted to the metal gurney, this body that

contains a body is wheeled
to the *delivery* room where the inner body will

be freed. Now no one
need say *push* because the urge to *bear down*,

to press for exit/entrance,
takes over room, light, breath—as though driven

to be turned inside-out,
laid open for the universe to witness *bairn* emerge

from a body that was *barren*,
resistant . . . but then the astonishing reversal—

don't push—words
shafting down a cool slide of light, this *don't*,

command the ardent body
can hardly bear, but voices insist: time to clear

the infant's head, ease it into this
world, to check position, limbs, egress, to free

the startled blue eyes,
nose, lips into warmed air—and then again, *push*,

so that the new form may fully
be discharged, may exit the womb's plentiful

blood garden—expelled,
sent out into the fallen unprotected world—and

the new creation laid
across the mother's breast, breasts to make a milk-

link between mother
and child, even though the first cord is cut,

remnants knotted to
a navel, mirror to the mother's, and link to every

navel and all cords
stretching back to the gates of that abandoned

Paradise, exile marked
by cord and cuttery, first of many leave-takings

dimly rising on horizon—
the child setting off to school or work or war, knapsack

stuffed with books and cautions,
perhaps prepared for the next and the next departures, which

can hardly—but must hardily—be *borne*.

FOLLOW-THROUGH

What is it about sticks and stones
and water that draws boys to the brink?

I watch my sons gravitate to cliff-
edge, stream-edge, stoop and gather

broken branches, rocks, hand-fit
and perfect to pitch into the current—

plunk, plunk—that tantalizing game
to make silver break to brilliant

flashes over river boulders scattered
by some larger gods, who plant in boys'

bones the hot desire to make
a mark on something. . . . My two

hunker down to gather ammo. Rise
to cock rock-loaded hands, then whip

forward, each perfect body thrown
wholly into *aim*. Such tender lines

of spine rise through supple skin . . .
baseball, I like to think—they study

strikes, practice for pitch and out.
I can be charmed by such relentless

intent because I've left the day's
paper crumpled back at camp—black

caption, black-and-white photograph—
the young man's body shot half-way

through that merciless arc. I do not
want to think my sons rehearse for days

when what they throw requires that
some pin be pulled, or gas-rag lit, or

53

missiles, perfect to the hand, be sent
into some other son's makeshift shed

or trench—muscles bunching fierce
into the follow-through that hurls

the packed device not toward surging
spray, but straight at that boy who'd

stood as they had—ankle-deep in joy,
under some other mother's watch,

in some other scintillating river.

PROPER

This plot is sacred. To our children,
    their beloved animals laid out
in makeshift shrouds of sheets,

cardboard boxes crayoned *Digger*.
    Flower. Beagle. Painted turtle.
Now, *Suzy*: kitty killed by the local

raccoon. Out of some dim ancestral
    sense of rite, the children direct us:
each adult in succession, each child

robed in chosen marks of sorrow—
    her unraveling winter scarf, his jean
jacket long outgrown, his thin wrists

shivering in the dawn breeze (dawn, so
    the animal's soul may ascend to what
the young ones have determined to be

Heaven). We've tramped through soaking
    autumn grasses to the almost-iced pond,
down the path they have laid out as

the proper way to go. We gather near
    the brink—useless as stones—while
they wield the unwieldy shovel, part

and pat the creek-bank dirt to make
    a fitting home from which the animal's
spirit might lift to blue fields above.

We check the urge to stroke the unbrushed
    tails of hair so close to our hands—
unwilling to distract them from their

crucial task. And we, we trust that if
    we serve as witness here, respectful
of their grief and formal plans, our own

plans will not go astray: we will never
    need to suit up, never need to follow
small named coffins down to dirt.

A Blessing,

they say, invoking that radiant
        litany as bandage. As balm. . . .
    Our feet obediently pressed

to scarred planks, we three wait
        on the petitioners' bench, eyes fixed
    on hands restless in our laps.

A low-railed fence, not unlike
        the highest altar's, separates
    the black-clad judge (whose tiny feet

barely graze the floor) from anyone's
        anger. Bewilderment. Tears. Her job
    is to sever. Us from our son.

Our son from home. To assign
        custody, the *legal keeping*
    of this child, over to the State:

the only path left to treatment,
        to a house of healing for his anarchy.
    Desperation. Fear.

He shifts beside me, and a slow wave
        of fourteen-year-old breath and heat
    washes my skin. The vibrato in the air—

his tremble? mine? . . . Child who
        tore from my body, who blooms
    now most beautiful. His lightning

mind, wired somehow awry, and so
        wilder than I will ever
    know how to be. . . . *Blessing*:

a word meant to heal
        with fragrant balsam oil, wrapped
    whitest cloth to protect from affliction.

The papers, the pen. They set them
        before us. When we sign (and only
    when we sign, a kind of purchased

indulgence for our sins),
        the State will make available
    help for healing, for that shaping

we have tried but have failed
        to deliver to this child, who
    wrenches every tether, who

invades with chaos our spent days.
        Dreams.... His reckless rebellion.
Our wire of despair.

Sign, they say, and point to the line.
        I wrap a shaking arm about
    his defiant shoulders. I write,

below his father's name, letters
        of my own that twist in ink, spelling

    failed mother   unworthy   shamed

A blessing, they'd said. From the Old
        English, *blētsian: blood*. From the Old
    French, *blecier*—meaning *casualty*.

Injury.
    Wound.

GASSED

at the Imperial War Museum, London
—John Singer Sargent (1918)

Pay your pound at the door, check
        your damp winter coat. Shoulder
                the knapsack—its red pad, pen,

its lipstick, its tourist's Underground
        Pass. Pass through the hollow whistle
                of down-flaming planes. Enter

the upper hall: *Gassed* glows
        for twenty merciless feet, bathed
                in the blare of its low, hard sun.

Aftermath: bandages binding
        every eye. Every man blinded
                in mustard gas. . . . Fresh

off the boat, detailed to document
        glory, Sargent alights here by
                chance, seizes charcoal and pad

to sketch bandage. Crutch. Crumpled
        flesh. To glean each mortal heap,
                wreck of one day's bloody ordinary

work. Returned, he will choose
        carmine to spatter body and brow.
                Arrange littered flesh as a frieze

in this field. Daub dun mud. Yellow
        blot: the orderly's cap as he guides
                nine ravaged men toward the out-

of-sight field hospital tent:
        dazed line inching past bodies
                propped on packs. Each other. On

mud-ground and board. As far as some
        eyes can see—the artist's,
                yours: these are *boys*,

each gas-lashed son instructed to cling
        to collar or shoulder of him
                who creeps, eye-struck, before. . . .

See how the artist's deft brush chills
        the sun, blurs the boot wobbling
                on pebble, the blindfolded boy,

foot lifted too high for the guessed
        step—who hovers, feeling
                for footing through limbo,

never to reach the ghost-walled
        tent. . . . And who are you, safe in unsplit
                shoes, to watch, cool at the edge,

judging figure and stroke—a guest
        assessing affliction? Is it *carmine*?
                or *flame* that tints your cheek? In

your knapsack—rubbing the cell,
        the red pen, the sketchbook, your
                scarlet facepaint, your Underground

Pass—a fist of loose coins shudders
        and glows. Some marked to buy
                butter. Some to buy arms:

weapons for children
                not yet too blinded to fire.

Yellow Jacket

You know them—prickly. Insolent. Quick
to take offense, they brook no interference.

Short-tempered threats to peace, they built
a layered paper hive here between our deck

and the rock retaining wall—snug hold
where no one could arrest their endless

duplication, black and yellow, double
wing and stinger. They swarmed our

summer feasts, dabbled dark feet in cut
peaches, red juice dripping from rare steak.

They had no right. . . . Only a December
smash would do—when lawn and hive lay

stunned in ice. Our tire iron shattered
those six-sided, intricately fashioned cells

that had held, as tissued boxes hold
hand-crafted Christmas ornaments, their

coiled bodies' beauty: gold-ringed eyes,
lace-membranous wings. The delicate arc

of paired antennae—gilded bands worked
cunningly across the jet. We thought

they slept inside, coiled body next to body—
slowed, chilled. Helpless. But about

the workers, we were wrong: long gone
from this nest, they'd left within—alone,

asleep—the young queen, waiting to be
sprung. We stopped her. And summer.

Simmer

Bent above the battered desk, I aim
to limn the long pure streak of white

that cuts through egg-blue dawn,
the birch's lace-serrated shadow

as leaves begin to knuckle under
to October—but at eye's edge,

in my safe room's shadows, lurk
the leash, the bitter wire, the hood

that flickers out of other shade. . . .
The bleak objects insist: they summon

the stained chair, the socket jammed
with wrenched light, the gasp of electricity

that simmers in the wall's innocent plug.
Common objects. Rope. Wire. Match.

Knife. Waiting ready-to-hand in every
everyday American home. . . . I too can

insist on innocence. Cannot be held
accountable for skewed use. *Others*

heft these tools in sweaty, sand-stung
palms, considering how each might best

be turned to terror. . . . Now I've said it:
how fear deforms object. Subject. How it

twists the blessing of stout wire tight about
the most delicate of human parts. How

the honed blade edges into flesh, leaving
scarlet glyphs carved on body. Beyond.

How the chair comes to weep its litany
of piss and blood. How the young girl

who crouched frightened in the belly
of the stripped cargo plane, how in her

mottled regulation camouflage she steps
from shadow into sun. She cuts the next

hood from a pattern frayed with use.
The stripped wire warms in her recruited

hands. Before me she tests the human
leash lightly in her palm. . . .

I open mine. The twisted rope burns.

Hostage Clock

When she is seized, her captors erase
the watch on her wrist to handless blur:
there is no tense to talk about this face.

Silenced. Bound. Tracks wiped of all trace.
Shut up in stone and gag, she's twice immured,
seized out of time her captors erase.

Her family weeps at home, a flood-lit place,
and prays for *are* and *will*, but waits on *were*:
they have no tense to talk about her face.

Above the ticking town, each mortar's blaze
times this shortest night. The deadline stirs.
Seized by their cause, her captors erase

morning to etch *mourning* on that gaze
they'd cut off from a future they abjure.
I have no tense to talk about this face

that floats on midnight screens in bruise and haze,
but pray for raid or mercy to deter
fate. When she was seized, her captors erased
safe. Look—*don't look*—too closely at this face.

The Coat

Alone in the locked closet, a coat
of stars hangs on wire. Shut up

in dark, the stars glitter, blaze
in color—blues and reds—purple,

pink, green. Infamous yellow.
Everyday names to signify

shame. The stars, broken
shapes, are skewed, barbed.

And the lining, it sparkles
with shards of swept-up

glass. Such a coat would sear
skin down to rib, wound bone.

Long ago, yesterday—now—
the winners thrust this coat

into the deepest closet. Fit
the door with lock and bolt.

Look—here in your bystander
hands, a key. Try it. The coat

fits itself to the occasion.
The wearer. It is your turn.

Five Ways to Wear the Balaclava

Have you shivered? Has sleet stung your face,
    numbed your chapped lips? Have you wished
        for the fleece of the family lamb that ran wild
    through rows of ripening apricot trees—fleece
        combed by the fire, spun on the ancient wheel?

All day, the covey of mothers murmurs and casts
    on the ninety loose stitches, singing the oldest
        songs as they loop the yarn double-rib (*knit two,*
purl two), making a helmet of wool to shield
        your face from invading cold. At the door, you

pause before boarding. Into your kit she tucks
    the color of pine forests at dusk, the new *balaclava*.
        Knit to protect the neck's nape, the ear's exposed
    swerve, cheeks your *mamulya* kissed when she saved
        your childhood fall, wrapped you in her heart.

While the train's uproar fades into the steppe,
    she thinks of ways you will wear it: cap to cover
        your head's crown, flesh over bone. As a folded
    scarf to caress your neck, warm the apple of Adam
        stuck in your throat. She imagines your convoy

paused at the border, late snow lashing as
    you cross into Slavyansk, Sevastopol, Balaklava—
        how you will pull up her knitting to shield your
    head. But you know also the two other ways
        to shape this cap. When under the not-moon you

and *you* creep into the town now held by what
    they have said are *rebels*—tug the dark fabric up
        to cover your mouth. Now, who could swear to
    who you might be? Who can say how your teeth
        gleam like wild dogs' as you flick off the safety?

Or, better, pull higher the cover your mother has
    knit out of her heart: even the shape of your nose
        might give you away. Only the eyes, which some
    may hold are the *soul's windows*, only the eyes
        are exposed. Eyes frozen as stones in a deep

winter pond. Now, anonymous, you may stalk
    each terrified street, swagger the scope past
        shattered glass, across cracked monuments.
    Sleek as a tank, you swivel for barricade, spot young
        foolhardy hands clutching a lit Molotov. Smash

in a suspect door, swing the gun hard before you—
    in this broken-open room, a woman, a fire, a stool,
        a glint in her lap. Her panicky hands drop the needles,
    the half-ribbed hat. The wool at her feet is the color
        of pine. Color of iron.
                Color of blood.

But You My Son

Because the drug that comes to *cure* you
swerves instead to *kill*—
anaphylaxis,

Greek that means *against protection*—
and because you, sleeping
lone in your dark

bed, are starting not to survive, vitals
slumping on a distant
monitor, life

swifting away, and because the nurse's
cell is calling, calling—
but you my son

are beyond picking up, you are *coding*,
heart-slacked, plugged
lungs crashing—

she gears through *stop* and flashing lights
to thrust the fail-safe key
into your apartment

lock, she bursts into the tossing dark
where the great factory
of your breath

is shutting down, stalling. Stopped.
She heels her hands at
diaphragm and ribs,

bearing down—*press, release, press*—
but you are not coming
back, do not want

to come back into your not-protected
body. She lifts the quick
needle, *epinephrine*,

to jump-start the heart—fingers the anti-
septic spot, and thrusts
the sharp straight

into that failed muscle, speeding vivid
liquid home, re-starting
the engine

that for ninety hissing seconds stopped.
Stopped. And you come
back, called out of

the amazing dream, out of *peace*,
blinking, waked—O dear
my son, from now

to ever you shall be heart-marked
where the shaft slid in
to deliver antidote,

to call you back into your life, into
the shine and flow of ordinary
oxygen and light.

Send

    —between Incheon and Jeju, South Korea
    April 16, 2014

The shots crack open
on the screen: six teenage boys
brace against an angled floor, arms thrust

for balance at ferry
wall and window, impermeable glass
that cannot be cracked. One can do nothing

but breathe
while the child clicks—clicked—
his phone to *photo*, snaps his classmate

propped on the sill,
legs blocked against tilt, head
turned as though waiting for his school bus,

late down the road.
Hands stuffed in his pockets,
life-jacket that will offer him *nothing* inside

the sloping boat. *Send*.
Another, prone on the raked
floor, lifts his phone to shoot down, past

naked feet,
at crush and clamor—still-
breathing bodies—boys, girls—heaped below.

Go, I want to say,
go. But know they will not.
Did not. They will wait, obeying the captain

who has told them
stay, even as he crouches
to leap from the tipped prow. A blitz

of photos flashes—
flashed—from the foundering
ship, past wavecrest and cloud-burst, bursting

inside unwary
screens at home. Only
imagine how in the next days—*for ever*—

mothers, fathers,
will return to these images,
magnifying glass fisted tight, not able

to say *for
certain* whether this
child leaning or bracing is *him, her, him,*

their last only
look. And to hold at bay what
keeps happening next: the children stopped

in these shots
are about to drown—
already are drowned—even as anyone—

you, me—
pauses on the frame.
I cannot *send* to erase this boy's nape, efface

the dim wrist
of that girl, each image a litany
of witness: *here am I. Remember me. Us.*

ACKNOWLEDGMENTS

Grateful acknowledgment is made to the editors of the following journals and presses for first publishing these poems or earlier versions of them:

823 on High. "We Who Attend Suspended." 2016.
Adanna. "Another Kind of Prayer" (as "Another Prayer"). 2013.
The American Journal of Poetry. "Echo Baby Blue." 2017.
Anthology of New England Poets. "Night Terrors." 2000.
The Bellingham Review. "Simmer." 2006. "Having Vanished." 2014.
Cascadia Review. "Follow-through." 2014.
Cave Wall. "Kneeling," "Sometimes." 2013.
Cider Press Review. "Cicatricula." 2007. "The Coat." 2010. "Apoptosis." 2018. "What Were You, Before." 2018.
Cutthroat. "Black Seed." 2009.
Dogwood. "Inflorescence." 2006. "Yellow Jacket." 2006. "*Gassed.*" 2007.
Forage Poetry. "Send." 2016.
Healing Muse. "But You, My Son" (as "Cardiac"). 2015.
HeartLodge. "Advice: to Demeter." 2008.
High Desert Journal. "Fields, Burning." 2008.
Margie: An American Journal of Poetry. "A Blessing." (2005).
Measure. "Proper." 2011.
Mom Egg Review. "Waiting Room." 2017.
Persimmon Tree. "Her Silence Is." 2009. "Hostage Clock." 2009.
Prairie Schooner. "Five Ways to Wear the Balaclava." 2014.
Rattle. "B-Word." 2016.
So To Speak. "Tomoko Uemura and Her Mother in the Bath" (as "Tomoko Uemura in Her Bath"). 2016.
Sow's Ear Poetry Review. "Ultra/Sounding" (as "Correspondence: to a Never-Girl"). 2003.
Valparaiso Poetry Review. "Yet Praise the Scar" (as "In Praise of the Scar"). 2016.

"Simmer" also appears in *I Go to the Ruined Place: Contemporary Poems in Defense of Global Human Rights* (Lost Horse Press, 2009). "Ultra/Sounding" also appears in *White Ink: Poems on Mothers and Motherhood* (as "Correspondence: to a Never-Girl" Demeter Press, 2007); "Listen" first appeared there.

"Another Kind of Prayer" (as "Another Prayer") also appears in *Forgetting Home: Poems about Alzheimer's* (Barefoot Muse Press, 2011).

"Her Silence Is" also appears in *Veils, Haloes, and Shackles: International Poetry on the Oppression and Empowerment of Women* (Kasva Press, 2016); "Resistance" (as "Against Knowing") first appears there. "Sometimes" also appears in *Capturing Shadows: Poetic Encounters along the Path of Grief and Loss* (University Professors Press, 2015). "Breast: Still" first appeared in the chapbook *Passion* (Defined Providence Press, 1999).

"Her Silence Is" and "Hostage Clock" received the 2009 *Persimmon Tree* Prize for Poetry. "B-Word" received *Rattle*'s "Poets Respond" Award (March 27, 2016).

...

And a deep bow to poetry friends, mentors, and places that have sustained and inspired me over the years while this book took shape:

> To Maxine Scates and her workshop poets, who have provided me with inspiration and valuable critiques and support over many years;

> To my sister/brother poets, members of the Skyhooks critique group: Marion Davidson, Kake Huck, John Martin, Ellen Waterston, Pam Mitchell, Jane Thielson, and Carol Barrett;

> To the gracious readers of many individual poems and of the manuscript-in-process: Penelope Scambly Schott, Dianne Stepp, Barbara Crooker, Megan Merchant, Colette Tennant, and Carol Barrett;

> To the supporters of and administrators at Playa, Hypatia-in-the-Woods, Caldera, and Soapstone, for blessed time and space to read and write and revise in places of quiet and inspiration;

> To the Deschutes Public Library, for offering me unlimited reading and invitations to hold poetry workshops; to Central Oregon Community College and especially to David Bilyeu, who arranged for me to serve as COCC's first Writer-in-Residence when I was unable to leave home while taking care of family;

To Oregon Literary Arts and to the Oregon Arts Commission for fellowships to support my work;

To Loretta Slepikas for her splendid author photograph;

To publisher Laura LeHew and Uttered Chaos for her enthusiastic acceptance of this manuscript and hours devoted to making it shine;

To Nancy Carol Moody and Quinton Hallett for gracious and unerring eyes ferreting out errors and polishing lines;

And always to my dearest Phillip and our wonderful blended family of sons and daughters.

Notes

"Apoptosis"

> Also known as "programmed cell death," in this case the shedding of the blood "blanket" prepared for a possible implanted embryo. "Apoptosis" stems from the Greek, meaning leaf-fall.

"Follow-through," "Night Terrors," "A Blessing," "Proper," and "But You My Son"

> For my sons.

"Waiting Room"

> Heather McGown, *Schooling* (Doubleday, 2001).

"B-Word"

> The quoted line ("Put a baby in a poem and watch it fall, like a stone through wet tissue") is from an online conversation between Joy Katz and Sarah Vap http://theconversant.org/?p=8890. The section on Brussels references the terrorist bombings of March 22, 2016.

"Having Vanished"

> The epigraph is from *The Gospel of St John, I:1*

"Black Seed"

> Based on the myth of Demeter (Greek goddess of grain, corn, harvest) and Persephone (her daughter by Zeus), seduced away by Hades, god of the underworld. The conventional view suggests an unwilling alliance, a welcome return.

"Kneeling"

> For my mother. "Ginger and Fred" is the dance partnership of Ginger Rogers and Fred Astaire in many 1930s and '40s movie musicals.

"Tomoko Uemura and Her Mother in the Bath"

> The photograph, by photojournalist W. Eugene Smith, was part of a piece written to expose the effects on humans by mercury and other chemicals irresponsibly released into the environment by a manufacturing company in Japan. Although the copyright was returned to the family to spare them public intrusion, it remains available on the web, a reminder that care must be taken.
>
> http://en.wikipedia.org/wiki/Tomoko_Uemura_in_Her_Bath
> http://en.wikipedia.org/wiki/Minamata_disease
> http://digitaljournalist.org/issue0007/hughes.htm

"Proper"

> The word also refers to a solemn event in the liturgy of a church.

"Simmer"

> The poem references the photographs of torture at Abu Ghraib.

"The Coat"

> Source for the images is the Holocaust of World War II, including the colored badges to indicate disparaged identity, and the destructive events of Kristallnacht.

"Five Ways to Wear the Balaclava"

> Russia invaded the Crimean region of Ukraine in March of 2014. *Mamulya* is an affectionate diminutive for "mother."

"*Send*"

> On April 16, 2014, a Korean ferry (*Sewol*), carrying hundreds of passengers, underwent a sharp turn and capsized, killing more than 300 people, including many teenage students. The students were urged to stay in place. The captain abandoned ship.

BIO

Judith H. Montgomery lives with her husband in Bend, Oregon. Her poems appear in *The Bellingham Review, Measure, Healing Muse, Prairie Schooner,* and *Tahoma Literary Review,* among other journals, as well as in a number of anthologies. She's been awarded fellowships in poetry from Literary Arts and the Oregon Arts Commission; residencies from Playa, Hypatia-in-the-Woods, Soapstone, and Caldera; and prizes from *The Bellingham Review, Persimmon Tree,* and elsewhere. Her first collection, *Passion,* won the Defined Providence Chapbook competition, and received the 2000 Oregon Book Award for poetry. Her second collection, *Red Jess,* appeared in 2006 from Cherry Grove Collections; her chapbook, *Pulse & Constellation,* was a finalist for the Finishing Line Press Competition and appeared in 2007 from the Press. She was the first Writer-in-Residence at Central Oregon Community College, teaches poetry workshops throughout Oregon, and is a frequent judge for poetry competitions. She holds a doctorate in American Literature from Syracuse University.

© Loretta Slepikas

Made in the USA
Columbia, SC
01 August 2018